**ANCHOR BOOKS**

ENRICHMENT IN VERSE

Edited by

Heather Killingray

First published in Great Britain in 1999 by
ANCHOR BOOKS
Remus House,
Coltsfoot Drive,
Woodston,
Peterborough, PE2 9JX
Telephone (01733) 898101

HB ISBN 1 85930 648 9
SB ISBN 1 85930 643 8

FOREWORD

Anchor Books is a small press, established in 1992, with the aim of promoting readable poetry to as wide an audience as possible.

We hope to establish an outlet for writers of poetry who may have struggled to see their work in print.

The poems presented here have been selected from many entries. Editing proved to be a difficult task and as the Editor, the final selection was mine.

I trust this selection will delight and please the authors and all those who enjoy reading poetry.

Heather Killingray
Editor

CONTENTS

FRIENDS

(Dedicated to Jen, Fliss, Claire, Is, Caroline, Daisy, Laura and Fran)

You are so important,
Important to me.
It feels like I
have known you for a lifetime
Friends, you rock.

You are really special,
The best friends ever,
Now,
You know what you mean to me.

The most important Girls
Ever!

Alexandra Byers

FROM CHARLETTE'S ARK TO JESUS CHRIST

Me and Bubbles are all but two now
It's been two short years since we met you,
But you are nineteen hundred and ninety-eight
That's an awful lot of years to do.

Gabrielle and Goldylocks
Hold a feather up to you,
Jessica still holds her Rose
While sad Sam cries to you.

Here inside our little home
Have houses, paintings gifts from you,
And all the animals are happy
When all the tears are over too.

But when it comes to Christmas day
Out come all the dolls to play
All the teddies sit to tea
Dumpy, Popet, Bubbles and me.

And we shall light the Christmas candles
And play some Christmas carols too
And this year's crib is in a boat,
Well didn't you come for fishermen too!

And we know Jesus Christ is busy
Especially on Christmas day,
But we'd like to invite you round to dinner
As honoured guest on Christmas day.

Charlette de Christi

THE CHRISTMAS DEDICATED TO EUGENE

Christmas tree with various gifts hanging around it.
We are lost . . . where are you . . . ?
Where every person is!
Do you remember?
Do you recollect?
It was Christmas
Covered all around with snow
That I and fellow youth
Celebrated with you
Xmas white Christmas
It was colourful
The dining room was thoroughly decorated
Alongside the house
We were smiling - cajoling
With plenty of various varied foods
Laid on the table
We all pulled crackers
Drank cold hot drinks
Laughed joked . . . laughter all around
Ate foods . . . looked at each other
By one another with gifts exchanged
Even in a way danced . . . in our looks
In our imagination
With mistletoe hanging from the roof.

Ghazanfer Eqbal

DEDICATED TO MY PETS

I have lots of pets,
One bird, four hamsters.
The bird, or should I say
Birds (I used to, anyway)
Because I used to have two,
But one passed away,
Last year. So now I have one.

Now to the hamsters.
I have four, yes, four.
One boy and three girls (yay)
The boy is an albino,
So he is white.
One girl is brown and white,
One is tan and white,
And the other is black,

Now to the names.
Hamsters: brown and white
is the mother Nibbles,
Tan is Bonus.
White is Titch.
Black is Nora.

Claire Dennis (10)

DEDICATION TO MY MUM

You are my friend,
You are like a sister to me,
You are my guardian,
You are my mum,
When I am sad you cheer me up,
When you are sad
I see if you are okay.

Lisa McGuinness (10)

DEDICATION TO MY DAD

He helps me with my homework,
He gets up early on Saturday,
To take me horse riding
And every time he goes shopping
He buys me a chocolate bar.
Sometimes he makes me wash the car.

George Thirkettle (10)

CHILDREN IN NEED

Children in need
We raise money for you,
All the money's just for you.
All in two pence pieces,
But they have all been counted up.

Wayne Wolstenholme (10)

A DEDICATION

Michael Owen he is so good at football,
He can tackle so well and no one can tackle him,
He gets the ball off the player,
He takes a good shot at the goalkeeper,
Sometimes he scores,
Sometimes he misses,
Sometimes he hits the post.

Deen Lawrence (10)

DEDICATION TO MRS MOULDER

Mrs Moulder you're so fine,
Especially when you're
Leading in our line,
You're so kind
I'm glad you're mine
Thank you
Mrs Moulder.

Matthew Ashman (10)

DEDICATED TO DAVID

David Beckham I think you're cool,
I think you're the best at football,
I think you can dodge all the defenders,
And I reckon you are simply the best
at free kicks,
Because you can swerve it in any
corner of the goal,
And your skill on your feet can dribble
past anyone,
Your crosses are the best to people like
Michael Owen.

Tony Thompson (11)

MY MUM
(This is a poem I would like to dedicate to my mum)

Mum, Mum you're always there,
Mum, Mum you never swear,
Mum, Mum I don't care,
Mum, Mum I'm losing hair,
But most of all I love you Mum.

Heather James (9)

MY MUM
(I would like to dedicate this poem to my mum)

You're loads of fun
But you don't know
How to run
I think you're sweet
And really neat
You get very stressed
And I know why
You do try
To be a good mum
Of course you are
'Cause you shine
Like the sun.

Emma Conium (10)

Dedicated To Denis Bergkamp

Denis you're the best midfielder around.
Denis you're good at shooting goals.
You score excellent goals
Smack straight past the keeper
You're the best.

Kevin Filmer (10)

DEDICATED TO MY NAN'S DOG

My nan's dog is Boney.
She eats and eats,
Her coat is shiny and black,
Her eyes are blue.

Shaune Carey (11)

I DEDICATE THIS POEM TO MY NAN

My nan is very funny,
But she embarrasses me too,
Please don't do it Nan,
I won't embarrass you.

Some of my friends laugh at me,
But I don't really care,
I still don't forgive you nan,
You need to be more rare.

Gemma Candy (11)

POETS SING THE BLUES
ME, YOU AND A *GIRL* CALLED SUE

Walked past your house this mornin' feelin' deep-down blue.
Yeah, passed your house this mornin', feelin' oh so blue.
Peered into your window, and saw you kissin' Sue!

Now Sue she was your woman. Then I came along.
She was your special woman, before I came along,
And you called *me* your true love. Poor Sue, you done her wrong.

Now I stand here a-weepin'. You tell me: 'Go away!
Stop standin' there a-weepin'.' OK I'll go away.
But tears will keep a-fallin', until my dyin' day . . .

Elizabeth Mark

OLE CHRISTMAS BLUES

I've got those Christmas blues,
Oh I've got those ole Christmas blues,
My job is on the line, rent is due,

Singing Christmas carols,
Singing jolly Christmas carols,
But the world just weighs me down, got the blues,

Shopping on a shoestring,
On a warn out tattered shoestring,
With Father Christmas smiling through my tears,

Landlord's looking for me,
Know the landlord's looking for me,
I got those good ole, Christmas blues.

Fiona Bower

PARTIAL BODYSNATCH BLUES

Woke up one morning, found the leg end gone,
Woke up one Sunday morning, and found the leg end gone,
But the memory, her memory lingers on.

Woke up next morning, found the arm end gone,
Woke up on Monday morning, and found the arm end gone,
Yes, the lower part, the lower part, there was none.

Woke up yet again, found the back end gone,
Woke up on Tuesday morning, and found the back end gone,
O Lord, how can I, Lord how can I carry on?

Woke up one more time, found the front bit gone,
Woke up on Wednesday morning, and found the front end gone,
What now will I rest, will I rest my head on?

Woke up this morning, found the head alone,
Woke up this Thursday morning, the head was left alone,
O Lord, how she did, Lord how she did nag and moan.

Paul A Reeves

To My Son Donald

I can't believe how time has flown,
Out of your teens and fully-grown.
Don't have to wipe your snotty nose.
Nor help you on with shoes and clothes.
Don't have to sing you songs each night.
Nor teach you how to fly a kite.
Don't have to nurse you when you're sick.
Nor tell you off for childish tricks.
Don't have to teach you right from wrong.
For now you are a man my son.
Yet still I miss that far off time.
And treasure memories left behind.
But I am proud to be your mum.
'Cause you are just a perfect son.

Penni Nicolson

WIFE LIFE

Women are gentle
Gentle souls
The women in your life

But the women put
Women expect of you
Souls of discontent

When you come
Before women you are
What do they see?

It's hard to imagine
Imagine how hard
You try to see

You try to see
And fail in what you do
You try for women

Women behind or in front
Up ahead women
You're trying

How many nights
Just how many
How often?

What has it been
I am asking
Trying to see

Mother
Grandmother
Sister

A wife would have been
Wife I never had
Wife I couldn't cope with

Simon Warren

DEAR GRANDCHILD

I often picture you going upstairs,
as you make your way to bed
After you have said your prayers,
remember what granddad said.

Close your eyes on Christmas Eve,
sleep the whole night through,
Santa visits all good children,
making all their dreams come true,

Don't forget to leave a mince pie,
Santa will find it, never fear,
And you will have a Merry Christmas,
and a wonderful Happy New Year.

Wenn-The-Penn

AUNT MARGARET

I still fondly remember, when I was a boy,
How a visit to Aunt Margaret's always filled me with joy,
And today I cherish the memories of precious times we shared,
When she showed such loving interest, and genuinely cared,
With nothing ever too much trouble, as kind things she would do,
Treating me like a son, instead of merely a nephew.

To Jack, Ruth and her boys, plus wider family
She gave of her very best, and unselfishly;
She was someone on whom they wholeheartedly could depend,
For, to their every need, she faithfully would attend;
Yes, her contribution was nothing short of immense,
As she made to each life such a vast difference.

And Christ's love, in her actions, she so richly did show
To all those crossing her path who the Saviour didn't know -
Kind, considerate and thoughtful towards any in need,
To those who found in Margaret a true friend indeed,
To whom she would, so willingly, reach out a helping hand,
Responding to situations she seemed always to understand.

She enriched and touched lives wherever she would go;
She was infinitely special, and I loved her so;
And, being my favourite aunt, I ne'er will forget her,
Though she's now in Christ's presence, which I know is far better,
Made perfectly happy and holy, in heavenly rest,
And God makes no mistakes - He only takes the best.

The parting is so painful, yet one thought helps us cope,
In that we sorrow not as others who sadly have no hope,
For, as a blood-bought child of God, she has found eternal gain,
Where God has wiped away every tear, and released her from pain,
And one day, with the Saviour, we'll see again her sweet face,
Enjoying together, with the ransomed, the riches of His grace.

Ian Caughey

DEDICATED TO

Show me this feeling and another way of life
One day at a time each slice by slice
I'm ready to give it my all
I do wanna stand by you nansi Joy Birdsall
I love you more than ever
You're very intelligent, computer minded, very clever
So a merry Christmas I say to you
Anytime I write you know it's true
We started off as a seed and our love it grew
To all new satisfying levels to put us on a high
We've got to steer our course if we wanna get by
Get by the sea where the water is so nice
You are the woman that is the spice of my life
Nansi, will you marry me will you be my wife
Happy Christmas and New Year oh yes you are my posh spice.

Simon Peter Dennis

DAYS GONE BY

I remember a tale my father told,
When he first started working.
It happened one day at the colliery,
Early one frosty morning.
At the pit top miners were queuing,
Ready to enter the cage.
Waiting anxiously also, were three boys,
Just fourteen years of age.
Now it was their turn to step inside,
The others joked away.
The operator too, had been told of,
The youngsters starting that day.
So he was ready to give them a ride,
One they would remember well.
He jerked the cage up, then let it drop,
Faster than usual it fell.
As the young boys screamed, and clung tightly,
The older men laughed aloud.
Making fun of the trembling youngsters,
Seeing them shaken and bowed.
Frighteningly, they plunged on downwards,
While dim light from their lamps
Lit a scene of flashing steelwork, and
Walls that were dark, and damp.
Would their journey ever end,
They wondered and they prayed.
At last, they arrived at the pit bottom,
Thankful their journey was made.
Still laughing, the older ones left them,
To recover from their ordeal.
Yes my father never forgot his ride,
That day in the cage on the wheel.

Terry Daley

CHRISTMASITIS

Christmas is a time of year
that usually delights us.
But each year recently
I've suffered from Christmasitis.
It spoils a lot for me and
particularly stops me coping.
I can't clean, can't cook,
it generally starts me moping.
The rest of the year
I can cook some marvellous meals.
Christmastime I lose the knack,
and fill the house with squeals.
I seem to worry more,
my head gets like a sieve.
It's really awful when one
is meeting a relative.
I'm glad it's over again for
another twelve months.
I'll go on holiday next year,
and enjoy myself for once.

Ann May Wallace

POLITENESS LENDS ITS EAR

Petulant actions to attract attention
Conditioned to react to many mannerisms
Listen out of politeness
Good or bad leaves lasting impression
One's own conclusion has final say
Psychological disorder erupts if one's unable to take hold
Which is frequently foretold.

Alan Jones

TROUBLED CONSCIENCE

Why worry about confessing your sins when you can go public on TV!
Your conscience is absolved by the applause of those, supping cold tea.
Cheating on your wife, by cavorting with her mum, rouses a loud cheer.
You may be invited back for public contrition before the end

of a year!

To visit a confession box and in darkness, confess to woeful misdeeds,
Why not, have a session with a psychiatrist, to sort out all your needs!
Lying on a couch you may release old troubles, floating off in bubbles.
A peaceful mind diminishes the urge to excel in sets of mixed doubles!

There was a time when the discontented mind was unable to find ease.
Wrapped in sacks and ashes outside a church, it crawled on its knees.
A public penance on high lofty steps made guilt and blame disappear.
Many showed the world that they were sorry; lesser men did but fear.

If your misdeeds were diabolical, you could churn out a splendid book.
Newspapers rush to torture you for the rights, at every indiscreet nook.
Film producers might screen that book and weave it into a blockbuster.
Never again for the rest of your life need you place a hand on a duster.

The media hosts you for acting badly but ignores you for being good.
So, if your crimes are weighing you down, now brighten up your mood!
Lift up your hand; dial the telephone for famed fortune lurks so near.
A staged or filmed presentation of your guilt, might be a 'hit' next year!

T Burke

THE OLD HOUSE

I wandered through the old house
where I had chanced to dwell,
and wondered, if these walls could speak,
what stories could they tell.

What kind of people lived here then?
Were they rich or poor?
Did they live a happy life,
those that paced this floor?

Did children play within these rooms,
and did their laughter ring?
Did their father, stories tell,
and did their mother, sing?

Did horse and carriage stop outside
whilst visitors called round?
Or was it just a lonely place,
a place without a sound?

Were children born, did others die?
And did they mourn their dead?
Did their bodies lie in state
stretched out upon their bed?

Did the swallow, then, as now,
with twigs and sticks, and leaves,
build its tiny little nest,
high up upon the eaves?

I wandered through the old house,
now rank, with musty smell,
and wondered if these walls could speak,
What stories *would* they tell?

E A Wade

SING THE BLUES

Pease pudding hot
Pease pudding cold
There was nothing in the pot
Or so we are told.
Times were very hard, there wasn't any work
Father couldn't put to sea
Oh dear me!

Hot cross buns, hot cross buns
One a penny, two a penny
Hot cross buns.
We listened at the keyhole
While Jimmy rang his bell
But there was nothing in the pot
Oh go to Hell!

Belly all a rumble
Baby screaming mad
Jimmy's basket full of bread, but that was sad.
Carol singers at the door
Belting out a tune
Singing 'Happy Christmas'
Mother all a fume.

No pease pudding hot?
No pease pudding cold?
That will never do the leader of the choir said,
Turning very blue.
Take what we've collected
This snowing Christmas Eve
Have not a hungry Christmas
Please, please, please!

P M Burton

SINGING '*THE BLUES*' AS I WRITE

I want to write a poem, to prove my love to you;
I want to write a poem, I don't know what to do;
I've *just* composed that poem, a stanza just for *you!*

Ron Allan

NO GOOD NEWS BLUES

You turn me blues,
you burn me blues,
why do I have to be in these shoes?
Oh blues, you ain't good news.

Once knew a woman
hair like gold
eyes like stars,
but her heart was cold.
She's in my mind
she's in my head
she used me up, left me for dead,
oh blues, you ain't good news.

Oh babe, sweet woman
my life's a sieve,
can't live without you, can't live with,
oh blues, you ain't good news.

Electric blues
shivering down,
down to my soul and round and round.
Oh blues, you ain't good news.

Pam Redmond

ELEGY ON A TREE

My branches droop through frost and rain,
the birds have all gone home again.

The wind feels colder round my trunk,
I clasp the earth with roots that dunk.

Into the pools of slimy mud,
waiting for spring to show a bud.

When all at once I hear a sound,
something has clasped my trunk around.

As sap runs down I fall in half a limbless
tree without a bark,
roots torn from earth take my last breath
no more will I be touched by lark.

Branches are all waving whispering a last
farewell,
this was a place where once we trees all
used to dwell.

Jean Paisley

GOOD AND BAD

She will always have
Good luck
Follow her all around
I will always have
Bad luck
Just walking into town
Lovely she shall
Always be
As radiant as the night
Ugly I shall
Always be
Insane and not so bright.

Philip Allen

FOR CARMEN

To you
I give health.

There is no need
to give anything
else.

You
had every quality
anyone
could ever
wish for.

Danielle Apap

An Eavesdropping Poem On The Tele

What if there's not, what if we only get one chance?
I'll have to talk with him in the morning.
You're really beautiful, do you know that?
It's junk mail probablys.
Yeah, that's exactly what it is.
For goodness sake love, it's not a football match!
Good morning sweetheart!
Well, so far so good.
No, I think I have had enough for the moment
I just took off without thinking.
Grief can make you do silly things sometimes.
Now might not be the right time to mention this, but,
I think we're going to die!

John Longford

EAVESDROPPING POEM ON A BUS

Hi'er love, Hi'er pet,
Eee, a heard Gary and Louise had a baby,
Ahh, a boy wasn't it.
My favourite's the ones with caramel.
Nah, they're *crap!*
A ya comin' out ta neet,
Nar,
But the graphics are mint
Oh, man, me yo-yo's bust
Ne point man
Like a pig, in a cage, on antibiotics
Yer, what.

J Dunbar

AN IMPOSSIBLE TASK!

How do flowers know, when it's time to grow?
My son asked this, but I didn't know,
And, where does the water go, when the tide goes out?
I hadn't a clue, without a doubt!

Why, do we have, ten fingers and toes?
And why, do rice fields grow in rows?
What, makes the world go round?
And why, can't we hear, a high pitched sound?

> The questions, kids ask,
> An impossible task!

Evelyne A McMaster

MARKET SATURATION

He lied to the Nation,
He lied to a friend,
He lied in Congress
Without reservation!
To every member,
Times without number;
To many or a few -
'There's no one left
For him to lie *to.'*

Tom Ritchie

THE STONE BRIDGE

To the right, hideaway houses,
To the left, a runaway road . . .

Day by day
stand at the centre
of the stone bridge to appreciate
a sweep of unrestricted sky.

Follow the progress of any cloud,
hesitant or fast-flowing,
whether overhead, or in the water
that chuckles below, before
hiding it under the arch
of the stone bridge.

Night by night
witness the moon turn its face,
change its shape, in cloud,
or out of it, glide through sky
or under the stone bridge.

But - do you remember,
that one day when, motionless,
against an empty sky, you stood,
staring down, at cloud massed, broken,
wind driven . . . and later, that moonless night,
saw the face of the full moon float
towards you in the midnight stream?
Aghast, you panicked, you hurried
downhill to the hideaway houses . . . and
fled the road that rose with the bridge
over the water and ran off to the left . . .

Chris Creedon

TO JOHN DIAMOND
TIMES COLUMNIST, EX-DJ

The dreidel spins
And, mute, proclaims
The spinner's fate
In nature's court
Where justice blindly rains
Alike on sinner
And on saint.

No judge nor jury
Charts the score
Of records past,
Convictions spent or
Guilt and innocence
But one sentence
Only to die for - Life.

Joan Woolard

THE SAVIOUR'S DAY

Bright halls bedecked with festive holly,
With mistletoe, and garlands gay.
Glad voices greeting friends and loved ones,
'Come! Join our joyous Christmas day!'
Small children with expensive presents
Bought as a substitute for love;
Not knowing of the Christmas message,
Of God's great gift from Heaven above.
Fat turkeys roasting, puddings steaming;
Spices from lands both far and near.
Cooks heaving sighs, and tiredly saying,
'Thank goodness it's just once a year!'
Sad children, homeless, cold and hungry
Gaze at windows as they pass.
'It's not our business, close the curtains.
Let's quaff another festive glass!'
From far away' the sounds of battle;
Man's inhumanity to man.
Cries of the wounded, fearful, dying;
'Twas ever thus since time began.
High up above, sweet angels weeping.
They hear the Saviour sadly say,
'Was it for this I gave my life's blood?
What have they done to this, My Day?'

Estalyn Wilkins

AN OLD TREE

I had an old tree in my garden.
It always reminded me of Christmas
And it always made me smile
I planted it when I was little.
My dad used to say that it was ugly
But I thought that it was the best thing in the world.
I'll never forget the day that my dad took that tree away,
boy did I go mad.
I cried my eyes out
and planted a pear seed.
It never was the same in my garden from that day on.

Nicola Kemp

THE WILLOW TREE

Where is he?
He's in the pub!
Why?
How do I know?
What?
It's up a tree?
How did it get there?
She bought it.
Where?
In the pub,
like I told you.
And he *scored!*
Who?
Me stupid!
Yea! Right.
He's always in that pub!
Which one?
The Willow Tree
Ahhhh.

Kris Carr

BUS STOP 'CHAT'

Excuse Do you know when the next bus will be?
Two minutes.
I won that share, how much? Not enough!
I bought it. Bought what? that game.
So when's this bus coming - eh?
Can you lend me 10p for my bus fare?
This bus better hurry up!
I need another £60 to buy my car - in cash.
Won't need this bus when I get £60.

Daniel Bell

TIME

If time were an ocean
Where would tomorrow lie,
Beneath the creamy clusters
Of waves which heave and sigh?

Rachael Jones

OH DEAR WHAT A YEAR

The year of the millennium,
The year I shall be sixty-four,
Oh dear I won't be able
To run and jump anymore
Where life could become
Such a bore, but that
Won't be for me, I don't
like spending much time on
my bum, because I am a
grandmum they have me
going from here to there
and maybe take me to see
the dome and then I'll wish
I was back home.

J Drury

DO NOT DISTURB

Can I go back? I try hard. No voice says 'Enter!'

But the lock was broken - smashed by my father once
when he chased me upstairs and I tried to gain sanctuary.
It's familiar territory, though only half-remembered:
overblown red roses still trail over the wallpaper I never liked -
finally they did change it.

And there's that battered bulk of a wardrobe (not so high now)
I used to jump from onto the bed: the eiderdown is green . . .
out of my depth now where he used to plunge on the green.

From the mantelpiece below which, on cold mornings, the child
once huddled, his grey flannel shirt spread like washing to the warmth,
I pick up a piece of bleached driftwood; then
an old scallop-shell he brought back from a holiday:
(memory within memory); it's a-swill with safety pins, brass buttons,
badges, foreign coins and other forgotten spoils.
Hold it carefully or it spills.

But soon someone is showing me the door.
Better go; gingerly tiptoe out. He is happier
to be left alone. And me? Just as mother always said:
'You must spend hours in that room of yours.
Doing nothing, I suppose.' True. And now I'm stalled - here,
on this draughty landing with some paltry salvage,
I see a *Do Not Disturb* sign hangs on his door.

Andrew Mayne

ASTON VILLA VS ATLETICO MADRID

One dark but warm Tuesday night
The sun has set, its warming rays alight.
The football teams are exercising,
Aston Villa are running and racing.

Atletico Madrid without Juninho,
Their fans chanting 'Atletico! Atletico!'
Both teams gather round to hear the team news,
Either side wanting to win and not to lose.

Atletico to get the thrilling match underway.
'There's only one team in Europe' the Villa fans say.
The ball's being passed here, there and everywhere.
Then Atletico score, their fans jumping in the air.

One half passed no change in the score,
Madrid and Villa both wanting one more.
In the dugout the subs keep warm all wanting to play,
Frustration for the Villa manager until one moment in the day.

Aston Villa win the free kick just outside the goal area,
Taylor to take the kick, is there a position more scarier;
He takes the kick oh what a bender what a goal!
Ian Taylor celebrating with a forward roll.

Two minutes from the goal of Ian Taylor,
With Julian Joachim showing his pace once more;
His pass to Stan Collymore who's through the defence.
Stan Collymore scores another goal of sense.

The ref looks at his watch, two minutes to go,
Those minutes full of passes, the final whistle he'll blow.
So the game is finished Atletico win,
Because of the away goals rule, we threw the game in the bin!

Matthew Birt (11)

THE BIG 40

You wake up on your birthday,
Think 'Oh no I'm getting old!'
Reached the dreaded fortieth,
Of which you have been told.
You say 'I will not panic,'
Nor will I make a fuss.'
It's only another birthday,
They come to all of us.

You look in the mirror,
What is that you see?
A grey hair standing out,
As bold as it can be.
Grey hair is becoming,
On some people that you see.
'That may be so,' You tell yourself,
'I bet it won't on me!'

You have come to the mid years of life,
No looking back on the past.
But try not to despair my dear,
The depression will not last.

Life begins at forty,
So I once was told.
Forget all thoughts and worries
About forty being old.
Enjoy yourself, go have some fun!
Because the years go swiftly,
Before you know where you are
You will be nearly fifty!

Pamela Rogers

WORDS

If only my words could express
the way I feel inside for you
then maybe you'd understand me
understand my words to be true

If only I could find the words
deep down from inside my heart
yet I feel scared to find them
scared that all you'll do is tear them apart.

Kaja Jarosz (15)

UNTITLED

I've been a daughter, a mother, a wife,
Hard work has always been my life,
So if I won the lottery, well
What would I do, it's hard to tell,

Travel the world, go on a cruise,
all the spare time there'd be to use,
give money away to charity
invite some pals round to tea,

But would I still have friends I ask,
or just people hiding behind a mask,
perhaps it would only be a sham,
so I think I'm better off as I am!

Linda Limbert

THE 'BRAT'

A most wonderful trip to Scotland,
but homeward bound trains did go awry,
a lateness affecting connections,
and causing the travellers to sigh.

Then low and behold an announcement,
a train although via different route;
pleased and smiling I quickly boarded,
seat near mother with toddler looking so cute.

All too soon though regretting such hurried and hasty venture,
child overtaking all proceedings, diminishing mum's ample stature,
an extremely noisy 'I want, want, want' were the orders,
what had this woman done to thus burden her shoulders?

A continual 'Give me a drink, give me sweets, give me *everything.*'
And although cajoling, tempting, pleading,
the unlistening brat totally and utterly ignoring.
In my childhood, for any youngster's misbehaviour,
maybe the remembered policeman's clip around ear,
or parental short sharp slap,
but then of course, no officialdom, 'Big Brother' or do-gooders,
                    making the parent take the rap!

Gail Weingartner

A Fairies' World

As I walk through the park blazing sunlight strikes the bare branches
                                                                    of trees,
icy wind whispers in my ears and whips my skin, sending goosepimples
                                    up my body, my cheeks begin to tingle.

I walk through an abundance of leaves,
Fantastic fire colours - red, yellow orange and green.
I kick them watching their shapes twist and swirl back to the ground.

Back home I see my hair is a mess and my cheeks are flushed from the
                                                           winter weather.
I watch from my window as slowly little snowflakes begin to fall and
                                              gradually ice the ground.
More and more cold snowflakes fall until everything has been touched.
All is sparkling and white as if transformed by fairies.

Then I find great peace and warmth in sitting by the fire, listening
                                                    to my cat purring
and thinking of the cold outside, where I am not.

Joanne Clarke

FISHERMAN'S BLUES

I took up angling when you went;
something to get me out, to fill
the empty hours and keep me occupied.

I see you in the growing flowers
along the river bank. My heart
has lost the strength it once had, to forget

that you were all to me. The fish
flash in the sunlit water like your eyes.
Wind brings your whispered nothings through

the leaves. The rippling water sighs
and races to the waiting tide; and I
cling to the ends of memories and dreams.

Dylan Pugh

THE DEMON COMPUTER

The demon computer has a mind of its own,
It sits in the corner until *I* come home
and want to write poetry, then enter *I* press
but all too soon I suffer distress.
'I can't find the file' and 'I don't know I exist'
It takes me a while to understand this
I get gobbledegook when *I* try to print
and finally it tells me 'I have run out of ink!'
The repair man called twice, a fortune it cost,
as soon as he left, I found all my files, lost!
The demon computer at random deletes
hours of work off *my* spreadsheets
'You cannot save changes to your poetry file'
So I have to switch off and come back in a while
but still no improvement, I'm stuck in this mess
Finally defeated, the off button I press
When I go back to my file it's lost all the data
So for Christmas I'll ask for a pen and some paper!

Paul Christopher Holland (12)

BERCEUSE

Hush, hush my little one:
        go to sleep. Soon
the sandman will build you
        a bridge to the moon.
Your mummy's gone shopping
        and left you with me:
she's buying a steak pie
        and hash-browns for tea.
Due to inclement weather,
        the football's postponed:
that's why I'm not playing.
        Your uncle has phoned
to say auntie's unwell,
        so they can't cope with you.
Your daddy's at home,
        having nothing to do
but care for his baby
        the whole afternoon,
while the sandman is building
        a bridge to the moon.
This evening, if Lady Luck
        smiles on your mummy,
she'll win a soft toy
        for her ray of sunshine,
condensed milk and honey
        to sweeten your dummy,
by getting four corners,
        a house or a line.
The fire makes me drowsy.
        I'm nodding off. Soon
I'll cross, like my baby,
        that bridge to the moon.

S P Emmerton

COUNTRY SINGING

Oh, you can't beat a country song
With good old country singers.
They know how to sing it out,
So join in and sing along.

Sing along, sing along.
Sing a little country song
With, of course, a country fiddle,
With, maybe, a acordeen twiddle
To make you sing along.
Sing along, sing along,
Sing a little country song,

Or, maybe, it's country dancing
Alone or in a square
To a good old country polka
At a good old county fair,

So dance along, dance along,
Dance to a little country song.
They know how to dance it out.
Better join in and dance along.

Bill West

THE SCHOOL PHOTO

'Our Sandra goes to private school
Show Mrs Blunt the photo, dear;
I love the uniform, don't you?
There's Sandra in the second year.
She's sitting next to Charlotte Pring,
you've heard of Richard Pring QC?
He drives a Daimler limousine.
My dear! They live in luxury.
And that's Samantha Featherstone,
lives with a wealthy maiden aunt;
her parents farm in Zambia,
her grannie was a debutante.
That's Katy Reeves. Would you believe
her mother was a beauty queen?
And next is Carol Medlycott,
the daughter of the Rural Dean.
And that's the Head, Miss Heavitree;
she keeps them under strictest rule,
much nicer than the children at
that awful Comprehensive School!
Your children must be quite grown up.
Are these their photos? May I see?
What handsome boys! You must be proud.
A daughter too, and where is she?'

'That's Jane, she is in London, a pharmacist at Bart's,
and Paul, now head of languages, he gained a first in arts.
That's Ben on Graduation Day, he did a PhD,
And there they are together, when at school, as you can see.

Yes, 'that awful Comprehensive School' in nineteen eighty- three.

Sidney Headley

THE HEDGE

Ten feet high; marked on the maps before Trafalgar,
When an orchard, rich in damsons, pears and apples,
Stood where the road is now.

This mass of privet, hawthorn, ivy intertwined
With honeysuckle, forms the modern boundary
Between neat village gardens.

Field mice scamper underneath, lively nest-builders;
Robins perch on top, sentries on watch for cats
Or crumbs thrown on birdtables;

Sometimes at dawn a shy dark-eyed deer will squeeze through,
Sabotage the roses, lick her petalled lips, then
Leap off down the stream.

A strong windbreak, protecting babies in their prams,
Grandparents in their deckchairs; a thick screen for lovers,
Dances, birthday parties.

Names like Nelson, Churchill, Ireland, Whittle, Dunkirk,
Fleming, Dickens, Elgar, Mafeking, Ruanda,
Swirl past in the breeze

Then die away. The hedge listens, absorbs, waiting
For the end of life, time and all boundaries.

Patricia Lucas

THE SEASONS' HUES

A kaleidoscope of colour
Of rustic autumn leaves
The change is so dramatic
From the many shades of green.

The hazy autumn sun
Filters through the mist
Sparkling jewels of garnet
And faded amethyst.

The changing seasons' hues
Shaken out of being
Tossed and blown through the air
From life itself they're fleeing.

A sea of crumpled gold
Ebbs and flows beneath our feet
Shrivelling, scrunched and trampled
Till the autumn falls complete.

Soon it will be winter
With trees in their dormant state
If they stand the test of winter
Then spring will rejuvenate.

Sylvia Radford

DEREK THE DINOSAUR

While waiting at the bus stop
For the number ninety-three,
A quite enormous creature
Came to join the queue with me.

'I've never seen an animal,'
I gulped, *'like you before.'*
'You must have done.' he grinned, and said,
I am a dinosaur!'

'A d-dinosaur?' I stuttered back,
Being taken by surprise.
'Oh yes.' he answered, modestly,
And filled his chest with pride.

Now dinosaurs, I had been taught,
Last roamed upon our Earth
At least a million years ago,
I'm sure, for what it's worth.

I therefore told him bluntly,
'Dinosaur, I really think
That creatures such as you, you know,
Are actually extinct!'

'Don't be absurd, you silly man!'
His voice was firm and true.
'My name is Derek, the dinosaur.
Do I look extinct to you?'

With several tons of solid flesh
Towering over me,
It didn't matter what I thought,
So I smiled, nervously.

Then I spied a box of popcorn
Which he held between his claw,
And asked, *'Excuse me, Derek,*
But what's the popcorn for?'

'Well, I'm going to the cinema.'
He explained as it got dark.
Then added, with a nudge and wink,
'To see Jurassic Park!'

A R Hawthorn

MY COUSIN DUSTY

My cousin Dusty, is a rock star,
at least he thinks he is.
He struts his stuff
at the holiday camp,
he's unbearably showbiz.

He'll practice on that guitar,
on the toilet, I'll be candid.
He'll strum the air,
he'll practice there,
but his playing's still bog standard.

He's looking for that record deal,
that'll get him dreamed-of riches.
Success this way -
he's drunk today,
and has been since the sixties.

He does the odd impersonation,
his voice warbles rather oddly.
His late-period Elvis
has no voice,
though is belly is suitably wobbly.

He'll constantly tell of the time
he met Mark Knofler backstage.
he told the star
they shared a calling,
and that he really didn't look his age.

He was not discomfited unduly,
when Knofler did not reply.
Dusty soon got over it.
Sobbing for only just an hour
over his lunch-time shepherd's pie.

David Baker

THE MILLENNIUM DOME

I'd like to see what's under the dome,
Is it full of little gnomes,
Toiling away at fever pitch,
So that it gets finished without a hitch,
All working day and night
I'm sure it will be a spectacular sight.

They are working on the rail line,
It's getting on for ninety nine,
Only a few hundred days to go,
Much to do, mustn't go slow.
People will come from far off lands,
To see the amazing wonderland.

Historic Greenwich is the place to be,
Plenty to do, plenty to see.
The queen's palace and Cutty Sark, and
Don't forget Greenwich Park.
The old Observatory, and Greenwich mean time,
You can even stand on the Meridian Line.
General Wolfe on statue high,
Has seen it all, with unflinching eye,
He has seen them cast the very first stone,
When they began to build, the Millennium Dome.

On that momentous day, when the time comes,
There will sure to be a roll of drums,
The corks will pop, and we will cheer,
For a very great and happy
          'Millennium New Year'.

Dulcie Beatrice Gillman

FIFTY NOT OUT

As I walk off the pitch,
the members of Lourdes
stand and applaud me.
Time for lunch.
It's not been easy.
Death's International Select XI
already hold
The Ashes
of several friends
Down Under.
But I'm still here
and after I have eaten
this oily fish and salad wholemeal bap
I'll return to the middle age,
ready to take guard again
and hopefully play
the innings of my life.

Dave Bryan

IN PRAISE OF A FORTIES LANDLADY
(A GOOD WOMAN IF EVER THERE WAS ONE)

I sing the praises of Able
(So jokingly called, her name being Baker),
And Able she certainly was -
Able to nurture and comfort a nervous young teacher,
Able to cosset her with home-made jam,
Able to nurse her through quinsies and boyfriends,
Able to listen to her tales out of school,
Able to wait up when I came home late,
Able to rise early when I went out before dawn.
The fastest producer of chips in the Midlands,
Steel helmeted in curlers like Pallas Athene,
My washing always perfectly laundered,
Pressed with an old iron heated on gas
And beeswaxed to smooth its movements.
Coal fires she had, like gigantic conflagrations,
Huge sizzling breakfasts she served,
'To give you something to work on, dear.'
Hot chocolate at night, cool lemonade in the summer -
Four years of spoiling I had
And took it all much for granted;
And then I flew the nest to marry
And lo, Able too found an admirer
Who took her off south, to a house on a hill
From where she could inspect the fleet, the gulls,
Ensuring they were all ship-shape and Bristol fashion.

Her life went well, until one day,
On climbing home to her beloved eyrie
Her heart gave out.

Fifty years on I bless her still
And in my mind she is as ever - Able!

Ruth Parker

HARLECH CASTLE

I came to look at you today
Your turrets strong and tall
And put my hands upon your slate
That made your thick grey wall
You've stood alone for many years
The centuries come and go
Standing there courageously
Fighting back the foe
Now the years have withered you
Your skyline has sadly gone
The once strong walls are crumbling
The enemy has finally won
So stand erect with dignity
Your standards blow on high
Amidst the pomp and ceremony
That in your history lie.

Fay H Lawless

LIFE IN A DAY

If my birth was this morn,
and my death should be tonight;
and my life here on Earth was
just morn until night.
How should I view the playthings
of the day, if in just a few hours
they would all pass away.

So if life on Earth is but a day
at school;
Should I play with the toys or
follow the golden rule.
For though it may be noon,
It will soon be night, and
all this life's toys will be far
from sight.

Bradford Owen Fatooros

POEMS FOR CASH

It's a good time to sell poetry books.
Literary suicide is always good for business;
it doesn't even have to be your own.

Perhaps I should invent a tortured soul:
angst in the laundry room;
death pushes the Hoover;
clouds hang over the changing mat,
giving a touch of pathos to my bare-bummed baby,
the potential orphan.
She has the requisite curls.

But then I would never get to spend the money,
and that would be a shame.
Why not buy my poems anyway
and let me drink Champagne?

Rosalind Hughes

HAPPY CHRISTMAS

Christmas is nearly here
Happy children full of cheer
Running happily, waiting to see
If Santa will bring special things for me
Smells of Christmas trees, holly and ivy
All the children are so lively,
Tinsel sparkles like glitter in the sky
People are laughing and telling a lie
When Santa comes it is time to sleep
Close your eyes and do not peep
Dream sweet thoughts till morning time comes
Of sweet dancing fairies and ripe sugar plums.

Charlotte Louise Hunter (11)

WHAT'S 'ER NAME

I'll read your poems later dear,
that's what he always said
as I offered sheaves of papers
to the back of his balding head.

He was like a permanent fixture
slumped before that TV set
and to think he was such a mobile bloke
years ago, when we first met.

I'll read them in a minute dear,
I must hear the final score
and I hammered harder on the keys
I'd heard it all before.

I'll read them all later dear
when the television's done,
the little white spot has not appeared
and I've a video to rerun.

But when I'm rich and famous
I can visualise his response
he'll lift his eyes from the TV Times
and say
I'm sure I knew that woman once.

Wilburt Wagtail

KING OF THE AIR

The eagle master of the sky
  seeks out its prey from up on high
Then hurtles down on mountain hare
  a poor victim who is so unaware

Then high upon a mountain peak
  he tears the hare with sharpened beak
Its hunger filled it takes the air
  with flying skills beyond compare

Up aloft in the heavens bright
  it is like an arrow in its flight
No other bird is so fast of wing
  the eagle is the king of kings.

Lachlan Taylor

QUIET MOMENTS

I have quiet moments to myself - it is a time when I think of past events
and future days that may come my way - how then will
I value the hours of each day - with this thought in mind - I try all
I can to enjoy the passing of my time on earth - and when moments
come to me - and I know they will - when I am feeling low - I pray let
me reflect on the good ones I have spent to date - the quiet moments
help me to work out how I feel - think about true values in my own life
and most of all - I gain heaven's prize of peace of mind within my
thoughts - in this busy world that seems to have no time - when asked
by close friends - do you enjoy your moments all alone - I have
no doubts - and answer yes indeed - it is a time I can be honest with
myself - I don't have to pretend in any way - or put myself on the spot -
or debate - whether I am in the right - and still I can make an honest
boast - that I am never alone - while I have the ways of Mother Nature's
peace all around - birds in skies to catch my gift of sight - flowers on
the earth to brighten up the hours in my days - quiet moments hold
a high value in my world - a world I enjoy to be living in - Amen.

Rowland Patrick Scannell

IN AGES PAST

I see a room, and in that room,
  There burned a cheery fire;
'Twas there we sang 'The morning bright',
  And clasped our hands, in prayer.

And when we quietly took our seats,
  A kindly face, smiled down;
Each one of us, would braver feel,
  To face the Great Unknown.

The clean smell, of a well-scrubbed floor,
  Plasticine on fingers -
The thrill of a new reading book,
  In memory, lingers.

The time, when innocence prevailed -
  No dread, or later fears;
Who would not change their life today,
  For simple, early years?

Elizabeth Harris

SATURDAY AFTERNOON

When I was young, and in my prime,
I used to run along the line,
Then the ball went out of play
I waved my flag, and said Hey! -
'It's not for you, . . . 'It's t'other way'
Well! . . . You've never heard the names he called me,
So in a flash I waved my flag -
And beckoned to the referee,
Across he came . . . it stopped the game,
'Now what's going on!' . . . It's him - what's his name?
'Did he call you that!'
Out came the yellow card,
'Shut up,' . . . don't walk away - Come here!
Out came another card, - you're off! It's red,
The game restarted without him, his head held low -
Talking to himself, what he said, I will never know,
His side, they lost, two goals to four.
That was several years ago;
Now I find myself too old 'To run the line'
My hair's now grey which once was gold
When I look in the mirror more lines I see -
And without my glasses on . . . I'm as blind as a bat,
I'm thinking 'Can this be me!'
When I walk, very slow I go
It's my damned old legs, they don't want to know,
But go to the match, for me's 'a must',
'Oh sod the walk!' . . . I'll catch a bus.
We'll all be there, on Saturday!

Leslie F Dukes

A GARDEN WINTER WONDERLAND

Rustic benches
Golden leaves in a heap
A layer of frosty white
Upon a lawn of green
Crispy cold
Bare trees stand
In a country garden
A winter wonderland.

Theresa Hartley

DECEMBER RAIN

The night sky was weeping
Shedding crystal-clear tears
Drop-by-drop sweeping
By storm's ignited spears.
Haggard trees shiver'd
Under each drop of rain,
Which descended like river
On drenched with water terrain.
Moon's face was wrapp'd by clouds,
Which in vain was trying
To smile on trembling woods
Which were drenched and crying.
But bright morning arose
With sun shining around
And dawn casting red roses
On fresh emerald ground . . .

Stainslaw Paul Dabrowski-Oakland

UNTITLED

One couldn't possibly imagine
What it is like to be alone,
Yet some of my days I walked
Bare foot through the snow.
How I am glad you are here by my side,
For one day I will be with you and our hearts will collide.

It's funny if you view life like I, as we grow old,
Because our lives are really like the snow.
It comes and goes and that one same snowflake will never return.

Yes, our lives are judged by the conditions of each individual day,
As we stand there watching it melt away.

Oh, I will soon come to you one day,
As I kneel down every night to honour and pray.
Then I awoke with the spirit of joy by my side!
But, 'Where am I?' I said to myself on this misty day?

Then a voice sang, 'Don't worry, look here's your wife.'
'See, you never gave up praying for the chance to be reunited on
Such a holy day!'

So we are now together, and in my future at last,
As I watch the freezing of my life now fade - and move - into the past!

'Merry Christmas to you all, because I got what I wanted!'
'How about you?'

Julius Edwards

CREATURE CREDENTIAL

On a warm summer day a crystal blue sky
a lone skylark song emulating from on high
The scent of the meadow with surrounding trees
this untouched corner of Kent to mine eyes it doth please
Amidst alone reflecting on what we have done
destroying life with spray pollution and gun
Nature design to cope for the need
but for man's insensitive lust and greed
On this planet long before humans arrived
nature's creatures and creations adequately survived
A furry bumble bee on her daily patrol
ripple in water marks the escape of the water vole
Birds take to the air with little fear
I wipe from my cheek their destiny tear
Man completely fails to see
with all his knowledge and technology
he will never rule supreme
having an attitude that's so mean
Nature will always override
man must fit in with his work and pride
We must be taking much more care
of all the creatures on land sea and air
Such a tragedy when nature wipes out hundreds of humans at a stroke
but who cries disaster for creatures in rainforest going up in smoke
We are given eyes to see such splendour
We are given hands to care and tender
We are given feet to go from place to place
We have a voice to shout loud disgrace
We have ears but to nature do we listen
alas no unlike money she has no need to glisten

We have a brain but fail to choose
right from wrong we just accuse
to love and care we just abuse
the world we share we just use
The sooner man is made aware of his task
to love and cherish and care
or is that far too much to ask.

H A S Beena

THE MORNING HORSEMAN

I rose on the wind from nothing.
I struck out through the pulsing air,
Over to that cross on the horizon,
That glints with the morning sun
On the place of the skull.
I took four winds for directions home.
I am the horseman of creation
That rode out from wonder, and nothing,
In the dark age of a pseudo-beginning.
Before first light, in a pinprick of matter,
I scattered out into the universe.
The smithereened stars, around me, shall testify to my journeys.
I rose from nothing, brighter than a quasar.
From a bright blue magical sky,
I rode down to deal out death to death itself.
I am the morning horseman, and you will remember me,
Under me sits restless redemption, and resurrection,
And I rose on the wind from nothing, I tell you.
I ran the race and won. I saw the symbols come undone.
I do believe I laughed once - long ago in a room of Nietzcheans.
I galloped hard through the wasteland world,
And never, brother, heard once *the word.*
I rose on the wind from nothing, my friend.
Brought into being with the bright light,
I have seen your concrete cities shine in the night,
And seen the steely flash of flick knives sparkles like stars
In the hands of vagabonds, thieves and villains.
Here let me introduce you all to someone;
Here pals, meet my good friend: *annihilation!*
I have far yet to go. Adios Amigo.

John Harkin

IT'S ONLY ROCK AND ROLL

Now they say that poetry's only rock and roll.
But when I told old Billy Blake
He just laughed that laugh of his
And talked about commitment,
Reminding me that Jerusalem
Told the horror of those days
Of Industrial Revolution
And in his Songs of Innocence.
He told of London's poor and plight,
They told of his commitment.
Now they say that poetry's only rock and roll.

Richard Reeve

SWANS, GEESE AND OLEANDERS

I stroll beneath the oleanders
And meditate on swans, not ganders,
Which drift around this little town
And tout for food till sun goes down.

For after all, what could be grander
On avenue of oleander
That here so plentifully grows
Than watching soft swans preen and doze?

I make my case with perfect candour,
Not blushing like an oleander,
That Sirmione's swans outshine
All other birds, however fine.

But Riva's streets and oleanders
Accompany, not swans, but ganders
As varied geese pursue their sport
And mow the grass around the fort.

This is no idle propaganda
For geese and swans and oleander
That line Lake Garda's sultry shores,
Since beauty is its own good cause.

Anne Sanderson

IMAGINING A DAY IN THE LIFE OF COLE PORTER

'Did I hear the phone ring?'
'Yes, it was Bing -
They need a song'
'When? - 'Before too long'
I read the story lines she's handed me,
Within the hour I would be
In a cab crossing town -
First get something written down;
Into my music room, closing the door,
Shutting out household noise, city roar;
My fingers reach for a minor key
There it is - the melody
Oh! Yes! Here come the words
Fine - just like homing birds;

'Cole, you old devil - where've you been,
We're working on the scene,'
'You have a problem?'
'Yeah, one or two of them,
The girl is beautiful but she can't sing,'
'That's going to be hard on Bing,'
'Cut! Quiet! We'll do an audition
Time for decision;
'Yeah! She is a beauty,
I'm praying I've done my duty;
They run through a time or two
Then, suddenly, silence across the set,
Their voices are blending, like velvet -
No worries now, not one bit -
We are in at the birth of a super, super hit.

Thomas C Ryemarsh

A HARD JOB

You were a funny thing, a spiv so neat and trim.
Clearing out your things is difficult,
First suit I found a watch, I thought 'twas
mine that you wanted to give as a gift.
Pockets searched in other suits will I ever
find my emerald ring?
I suppose I was fussy too, it clashed with
my outfit and was put in safe keeping
in the pocket of your suit.
How many years ago was that?
This is a hard job, I just got an odd look
from our eldest son as I'm sorting your stuff
into black bags to place them by the bins,
they served their time well.
Will I ever find my ring.
You could not throw anything out, now it's
so very hard to do,
For me to have a little space.
My Gentle Sweet Gent.

Margaret Gleeson Spanos

THE CONTENTIOUS COUPLE

Said a wife to her husband,
'A woman my dear
Is strong and wise and always sincere.
She is loving and caring with a natural wit,
And a funny remark for occasion to fit.'

'She will make you her world giving all it entails,
Happiness for eternity her presence unveils.
To provide all the tenderness a man will need,
And nourish with love she will forever feed.'

'But to cheat on a woman wise it is not,
And to abuse her will land you in waters hot.
For a woman my dear as I said is strong,
And her wrath inflicts pain that no court will rule wrong.'

Said a husband to his wife,
'but a man my sweet,
Is stronger and wiser less prone to defeat.
He protects a woman and her delicate ways,
As she serves and protects him throughout her days.'

'He is strong as an ox with a brilliant mind,
A superior brain and each is one of a kind.
Of course the world does revolve around him,
For a man was here first and forever he'll live.'

'Please do as I say take your foot from my crotch,
To calm my nerves bring me a double scotch.
I'm sorry I called you the weaker sex,
Please untie my hands from that iron flex.'

Mia-Joy

TAIL-END CHARLIE

As down to my turret I wend my way
Is tonight the night I hope and pray
That once again we'll get back home
To see the lights of our aerodrome

We've passed the point of no return
There's another gone down we saw it burn
Their number came up is what they'll say
As we press on to make them pay

It's been a long night, I've got tired eyes
Twisting and turning whilst searching the skies
I hope that's not the fighter coming back
I thank the Lord 'twas only flack

Just an hour or two more to our eta
With luck we'll get back before break of day
It's a day off tomorrow all being well
Unless some poor devil's been shot to hell

For there's just a chance, the luck of the draw
We'll be put on standby, our days off no more
We're given no chance to put up a fight
When told here's your target for tonight.

James K Kernahan

HALLOWE'EN THROUGH THE EYES OF A PENSIONER

I've heard it all before, trick or treat
Have I any money, or even a sweet?
With my low income how do I pay my bills?
It's harder than you think with my physical ills
I struggle to the post office on a stick
It's really hard going, I'm not playing any trick
Getting my shopping is difficult too
Our bus service wouldn't serve a gnu
My daughter has to get my groceries for me
Else I'd have nothing to eat, you can see
I'm a frail old person with hardly two pennies to
put together
When you come every year I'm at the end of my tether
One day, don't forget you'll be old
Sitting by the fire, trying to conquer the cold
I don't need your tricks, what you say's bad enough
Old age is decidedly tough!

P Edwards

MY NEW LIFE

In 1999 I am going to change
Change the way I live my life
Try to make it better
Free from anguish and the strife

I am quite disabled
Have been for sometime
But I can see, talk and hear
There's a place for me somewhere

I shall not hide away
Wasting all my day
But I shall help other folk
Who are much worse than me

By helping other people
If only by writing letters
I can widen up their world
Make them feel much better

And, by doing that
It will make me feel
That all is not so black
As it used to be

So roll on this new year
I've bought new paper and pens
I am looking forward
My new life to begin.

Jenny Campling

STEPHEN

So many years have passed away,
Did no one know where you lay,
Cut down in the prime of life,
Leaving small children and a wife.
The familiar telegram that day,
One small child was heard to say,
Why did our Dad go away.

They did not come back down our street,
The womenfolk, no time to weep,
No time to mourn or the luxury of grief,
Mouths to feed and clothes to wash,
So please forgive them if they forgot.

But now we know where you are,
Laid down in that foreign field,
So near and yet so far.
We can at last say our fond farewell,
We can say our last goodbye,
Tears are futile now and words do not convey,
How very much we owe to you for giving us this day.

Sylvia A Phillips

WISH YOU WERE HERE?

Sitting in the sun
Loafing on a lounger.
With no one around
Just me and the heat.

I look at the people passing me by
People pass me in bikinis and trunks
They don't understand the hot blazing sun
And what it has to teach to us.

Put on your factor he says
Four would be nice
I reflect off it you see
Like water to ice.

If you don't get it high
then I'm afraid you'll be burnt
Your skin will start to peel
Like a banana in its skin.

So next time you're out there
Cream has the answer
Unless you want to end up with skin cancer.

Kelly O'Donnell (13)

A FRIEND

A friend is very special indeed,
A friend is close to your heart.
A friend is always there for you,
In your life, they play an important part.
A friend is someone that you cherish,
Someone you love very much.
Even though you may drift across the globe,
Friends will always keep in touch.
A friend will listen to your problems,
And lend a shoulder for you to cry.
A friend will always be honest with you,
They would never tell you a lie.
A friend can only be one of a kind,
And I think you are the one for me.
Friends for many years to come,
Hopefully that will be you and me.

Evelyn O'Donnell

GOD'S STAIRWAY

Across the snow-covered jagged stairway,
of the mountains in the sky.
The beauty of its wonders,
as cascading streams flow down.
Feeding green covered valleys
bringing snowdrops whiten crowns.
The wonders of His making,
never ceasing to display,
the power of the Great one,
in this wondrous pleasing way.

V N King

A SCOTTISH LASS
(A welsh man and a native of Beaumaris, Anglesey)

A bonnie Scottish lass working for BT
Was on the telephone speaking to me
I knew she was kind, by the way she spoke
She spoke in a broad Scottish accent, no joke
Speaking from her heart in a heavenly way
don't you say that phoning by BT does not pay
I would say she was advertising for BT, first class
She was really well suited for the job, my sweet Scottish lass
I have an idea what she was on about, but I was too slow
She was well informed and got the message across, and glow
BT look after this lady for her loyalty to you
Her voice was like music in my ears, birds singing and pigeons' coo
Before my stroke, I used to carve wood, but lost the use of my
right hand
My speech was also affected, I tried to write with my left hand
I have started to print what I want to say and think
My spelling is getting better and my words are the right way
around, wink
But my bonnie Scottish lass is right on the ball
So listen to me BT users go on using their service one and all
BT can give you a service that is of the best
Miss or Mrs Marge? Rooney I must confess
Her manner was quite prim and proper
I can remember her voice, it was so super
I have made up about forty odd poems about various subjects
Perhaps some day with luck get them published, with prospects
I have written these few lines in praise of a Scottish lass
Her voice and accent bowled me over and the feeling will not pass.

R T Owen

THEY CAME THROUGH

Some soldiers gave us their sweets
Took us to cinema or a dance for a treat.
We did not have a lot of time
Most of us had to be in by nine.
There was always news of the war
People sleeping in shelters on a damp floor.
We had a lot of evaccuees to find a home
Most went to people living alone.
Some had no clothes and were unwell.
A lot of their memories they would tell.
In the school hall they first were fed
When they were bathed - they were given a bed
Some tried to run away
In the country they did not want to stay
God gave us His blessing, the war was over.
And with His help a lot recovered.

Margaret Upson

RAIN

Rain, rain,
Go away,
Come and visit early May,

You're so cruel,
You're so bad,
I wish I could be a little mad,

I'll sit there for hours and hours,
watching you use your selfish powers,
But instead I'll go outside,

Jumping and splashing,
running and playing,
and skipping and dancing,

I've learnt a lesson,
and I'm glad,
I've learnt that,
Rain isn't so bad.

Sonya Nikolosina (10)

ACHING
(Dedicated to my daughter Amy)

My arms are aching
My heart even more
For the little girl I've lost
My beautiful daughter I adore.

Maria Wadrop

TICKETS PLEASE

As they laugh I should be happy
For I am a passenger here.
I have paid to be amongst them
And they like me, it's clear.
But as my smile broadens
My heart takes another twist,
My ticket may not be valid
Should I move to another seat?

As they observe the landscape
I observe them
For I am on the outside
And inside lives my pain
I am momentarily distracted;
Passenger Twenty C.
New to town and possibilities,
Of guiding me to free.

Tickets please, confirm yourself,
I slowly show my hand,
Twenty C is more forthright
And not what I had planned.
So I return to making them laugh
Accepting their warm embrace,
But I get off at another station
No truth showing in my face . . .

Karen Hoyle

DANCING FOR THE MOON

Living through long years as a growing child
I loved to climb trees and play in the sun
I wondered if at night the moon shines wild.

My aim for admiration wouldn't yield;
sisters, tearing hair, must not be done.
Living through long years as a growing child.

Comfort from sibling conflict has the shield
of family. I cartwheeled before them.
I wondered if at night the moon shines wild.

Working hard at school my nature grew mild.
Daily I raced through set work, cards of sums -
living through long years as a growing child.

Came the joy of dancing class, pleasures piled,
magic as moonlight glowed because I'd won.
I wondered if at night the moon shines wild.

Dancing through Life's impossibly beguiled,
there will be sad times as well as fun.
Living through long years as a growing child
I wondered if at night the moon shines wild.

Geraldine Bruce

THE MARVELLOUS MCGANNS

There must be a factory somewhere
Manufacturing McGann's
They've got so many of them now
They've had to form a band

I say it's time to make a stand
It's time to strike a blow
Before they get the upper hand
And make another Joe

A proper Charlie I would feel
If we let these Brylcream Boys
Continue manufacturing
All these Dr Who decoys

It's time for sabotage I feel
We need a volunteer
With or without a monocle
To be our mutineer

There's a cold wind blowing
Mark, our mission cannot fail
For the cold wind that is blowing
is known as the Hanging Gale.

David Carton

Humour In Verse

There was an old man from Peru
who bent down to lace up his shoe
there was pain in his eyes
when he couldn't arise
so they folded him neatly in two.

There was a young fellow from Kent
whose head had a funny shaped dent
a misguided lark
settled there in the dark
and twittered to mark the event.

Jonathan Bryant

I SHOULD'VE GONE TO YOGA

I should've gone to Yoga
But the ogre Poetry kept picking on me.
It bugged me in the bathroom,
It tied me to the bed,
It made me see a theme
In the steam from my cup of tea,
It chased me round my head.

Lost were the postures
Last fostered a week ago,
Gone were the balance and the breathing technique.
'I've got you where I want you!'
Grinned the ogre 'I'm fond of you.'
And in came the rhythm and creative mystique.

We dropped crumbs to the drums
Of a nice little triolet
Then wrote most after toast and a quick quatrain.
'I told you,' said the ogre,
'Relax - it's nearly over -
Now how about a sonnet or at least a douzain?'

It was much too late to meditate
But dedicate this rhyme I must
To the sacrificial Yoga
And good intentions left for dead.
It was too late now for Yoga,
Drowning in poetic lust,
So I went shopping instead.

Sandra Kershaw